Table o

Author's Afterthoughts

25 Delicious Haitian Recipes

(1) Haitian Style French Toast

If you are looking for a healthy and delicious breakfast dish to enjoy, then this is the perfect dish for you. Serve this for breakfast or for brunch to make a dish you won't soon forget. For the tastiest results I highly recommend serving this dish with some grilled veggies and a cold glass of champagne.

Serving Sizes: 6 Servings

Cooking Time: 20 Minutes

Ingredient List:

- 1 Baguette, French Variety
- 1 Cup of Orange Juice, Fresh
- ½ Cup of Whipping Cream, Heavy Variety
- 2 Eggs, Large in Size and Beaten
- 1 teaspoon of Cinnamon, Ground
- ¼ Cup of Sugar, White in Color
- Dash of Nutmeg, Ground
- 3 Tablespoon of Butter, Soft
- 2 Tablespoon of Sugar, Confectioner's Variety

Instructions:

1. Cut the ends of your loaf off and make sure to reserve for later use.

2. Then cut your loaf into thick slices. Allow to stand overnight.

3. Then use a medium sized baking dish and combine your fresh orange juice, whipping creams, beaten eggs, cinnamon and sugar until thoroughly combined.

4. Place your bread slices into your dish and allow to soak for the next 5 minutes.

5. Next use a large sized skillet and melt your butter over medium heat. Once the butter has melted add in your bread slices and cook until brown in color on both sides. This should take at least 5 to 10 minutes.

6. Serve with a dusting of confectioner's sugar and enjoy right away.

(2) Traditional Beef Liver and Onions

In Haiti, you will find beef cooked on virtually everything and you will usually find every part of the cow used in this cuisine. Nothing goes to waste and this recipe is a perfect example of that. This dish is unique in taste and incredibly healthy for you.

Serving Sizes: 2 Servings

Cooking Time: 35 Minutes

Ingredient List:

- 1 Pound of Liver, Beef Variety
- ¼ Cup of Onions, Finely Chopped
- 3 Limes, Fresh and Juice Only
- ½ teaspoon of Salt, For Taste
- 3 Tablespoon of Vinegar, White in Color
- ¼ Cup of Oil, Vegetable Variety
- 2 Tablespoon of Tomato Paste
- ½ Cup of Water, Warm
- 3 Tablespoon of Haitian Seasoning

Instructions:

1. The first thing that you will want to do is bring a large sized pot of water to a boil over medium to high heat.

2. While your water is boiling, place your beef liver into a large sized bowl and pour your lime juice over it. Stir thoroughly to coat.

3. Next take some boiling water and blanch it quickly by pouring it over your liver. After a few seconds strain the liver and add in your Haitian seasoning. Allow to marinate for the next 15 minutes.

4. Then use a large sized skillet and heat up some oil over medium to high heat. Add in your beef liver and cook until golden brown in color.

5. Add in your tomato paste, onions and at least ½ cup of your boiling water to your skillet. Cook for at least 5 to 7 minutes.

6. Season with some salt and remove from heat.

7. Serve with your favorite sides and enjoy.

(3) Savory Pumpkin Soup

Here is a dish that you can serve up whenever pumpkins come into season. For the ultimate Haitian dining experience, I highly recommend serving this dis in a cleaned pumpkin shell.

Serving Sizes: 8 Servings

Cooking Time: 1 Hour and 30 Minutes

Ingredient List:

- 1 Pound of Beef, Lean
- ½ Cup of Olive Oil, Extra Virgin Variety
- Some Water, As Needed
- 1 Scallions, Large in Size and Finely Diced
- 1 Cabbage, Medium in Size, Half and Roughly Diced
- 2 Potatoes, Peeled and Finely Chopped
- 2 Yams, Peeled and Finely Chopped
- 2 Malanga, Peeled and Finely Chopped
- 2 Pumpkin, Peeled and Chopped
- 2 Turnips, Peeled and Finely Chopped
- 3 Carrots, Medium in Size and Finely Chopped
- 1 Stalk of Celery, Fresh and Diced
- 1, 6 Ounce Pack of Spaghetti, Thin Variety
- 1 Tablespoon of Tomato Paste
- 1 Pepper, Scotch Bonnet Variety
- 5 Cloves, Crushed
- 4 Sprigs of Parsley, Fresh and Roughly Chopped
- 1 teaspoon of Black Pepper, For Taste
- 1 teaspoon of Thyme, Fresh
- 2 Shallots, Finely Diced
- 1 teaspoon of Salt, Seasoning Variety and for Taste
- 2 Cubes of Chicken Bouillon

- 1 teaspoon of Garlic, Powdered Variety
- 1 teaspoon of Onion, Powdered Variety

IIIIIIIIIIIIIIIIIIIIIIIIIIIIIIIIIIIIIIIIIIIIIIIIIIIIIIIIIIIIII

Instructions:

1. First mix together your seasoning salt, powdered garlic and onion and chicken bouillon cubes and rub this mixture over your meat. Allow to marinate in your fridge for at least 1 hour.

2. After this time place your seasoned meat into a large sized stockpot and cover with enough water. Add in your oil and allow your mixture to boil over high heat. Boil until your water has fully evaporated. Then reduce the heat to a simmer and allow to simmer until your mixture is brown in color.

3. Add in your tomato paste and stir thoroughly to combine. Remove from your pot and set aside for later use.

4. Next add in your scallions and onions into your stock pot with a touch of oil. Stir thoroughly and continue to cook until your onions are translucent.

5. Add in your potatoes, yams, pumpkin, Malanga, carrots and turnips. Stir to combine and add in your cabbage. Stir again.

6. Add in your water and bonnet pepper. Season with your cloves.

7. Cover and allow to cook over medium to high heat for the next 45 minutes to an hour or until your vegetables are tender to the touch.

8. Remove your pumpkin from your pot and add to a food processor. Blend on the highest setting until thoroughly pureed. Add back to your pot along with your meat.

9. Add in your thyme, spaghetti and parsley. Add enough water to cover and allow to cook until your pasta and meat are tender to the touch.

10. Remove from heat and serve while still piping hot.

(4) Tasty Spinach and Cornmeal

This delicious dish is the equivalent to breakfast style grits. This delicious Haitian meal is typically served for breakfast and can be served with a side of avocados to garner the tastiest results.

Serving Sizes: 2 Servings

Cooking Time: 25 Minutes

Ingredient List:

- 2 Cups of Cornmeal, Coarse Variety
- 2 Cups of Spinach, Roughly Chopped
- ½ of a Tomato, Finely Diced
- ½ of an Onion, Finely Diced
- 1 teaspoon of Seasoning, All Purpose Variety
- 1 Cube of Chicken Bouillon
- 1 teaspoon of Salt, For Taste
- 2 Tablespoon of Olive Oil, Extra Virgin Variety
- 1 Tablespoon of Tomato Paste
- 2 Cups of Water, Warm

IIIIIIIIIIIIIIIIIIIIIIIIIIIIIIIIIIIIIIIIIIIIIIIIIIIIIIIIIII

Instructions:

1. Use a medium sized pot and add in your olive oil. Heat over medium heat and once the oil is hot enough add in your onions and tomatoes. Cook until your onions are translucent.

2. Then add in your chicken bouillon and stir thoroughly until it fully dissolves.

3. Next add in your spinach and continue to stir until thoroughly combined.

4. Add in your warm water and tomato paste.

5. Increase the heat to high and bring your mixture to a boil. Season with some salt before adding in your cornmeal. Stir and allow to cook for at least 5 minutes.

6. After this time reduce the heat to low and cover. Continue to cook for the

next 15 minutes. Make sure that you stir once in a while to prevent burning and clumping.

7. Remove from heat and serve with a few slices of avocado. Enjoy while still piping hot.

(5) Tasty Haitian Sauce

This is a sauce recipe that I know you are going to want to serve with nearly every other Haitian dish you make. Best when served with pork or chicken dishes, this will add a more unique and exotic flavor to every dish that you make.

Serving Sizes: 2 Servings

Cooking Time: 20 Minutes

Ingredient List:

- 1 ½ Tablespoon of Tomato Paste
- 2 ½ Cups of Water, Warm
- 1 Tablespoon Plus 1 teaspoon of Epis
- ½ Tablespoon of Lemon Juice, Fresh
- 3 Cloves, Powdered Variety
- 2 Sprigs of Thyme, Fresh
- 1 teaspoon of Salt, Seasoned Variety
- 2 Tablespoon of Oil, Vegetable Variety
- ½ Cup of Bell Peppers, Red in Color and Thinly Sliced
- ½ Cup of Onion, Thinly Sliced
- 1 Pepper, Scotch Bonnet Variety and Optional

Instructions:

1. First add your water, tomato paste, vegetable oil, epis and seasoned salt into a large sized pot. Stir well to combine and set over medium heat.

2. Bring your mixture to a boil.

3. Once your mixture is boiling add in your cloves, thyme, lemon juice and diced peppers. Stir to thoroughly combine.

4. Add in your onions and bonnet pepper if you are using it. Stir again to combine.

5. Reduce the heat to low and allow to simmer for the next 5 minutes before removing from heat. Serve while still hot and enjoy.

(6) Haitian Style Spaghetti

This dish, also known as Espageti, is usually served with hot dogs, sausage or smoked herring to make a dish you will never forget. Feel free to serve this dish for breakfast or lunch. Regardless, I know you are going to love it.

Serving Sizes: 4 Servings

Cooking Time: 30 Minutes

Ingredient List:

- 1 Pound of Spaghetti, Thin Variety
- ½ Pound of Pork Sausage, Spicy Variety
- 1 Onion, Small in Size and Thinly Sliced
- ½ of a Bell Pepper, Green in Color and Finely Diced
- 2 Tablespoon of Tomato Paste
- 1 Cube of Chicken Bouillon
- ½ of a Pepper, Scotch and Bonnet Variety and Minced
- 1 Tablespoon of Seasoning, All Purpose Variety
- 2 Sprigs of Thyme, Fresh
- 1 Cube of Chicken Bouillon
- 2 Tablespoon of Olive Oil, Extra Virgin Variety
- 4 Cups of Water, Warm
- 3 teaspoons of Salt, For Taste

IIIIIIIIIIIIIIIIIIIIIIIIIIIIIIIIIIIIIIIIIIIIIIIIIIIIIIIIIIIIIII

Instructions:

1. First use a large sized pot and add in your water and olive oil. Heat over medium to high heat and bring this to a boil.

2. Once your water is boiling add in your spaghetti and cook until tender to the touch. This should take at least 5 to 8 minutes. Once tender drain your spaghetti and set aside for later use.

3. Next use a large sized skillet and set over medium heat. Add in your oil and once the oil is hot enough add in your sausage. Cook for at least 2 to 3 minutes.

4. Then add in your tomato paste, peppers, fresh thyme, chicken bouillon, scotch pepper and onions. Stir to thoroughly combine and cook for the next 2 to 3 minutes.

5. Add in your water and bring this mixture to a boil.

6. Once your mixture is boiling add in your cooked spaghetti and toss thoroughly to mix together.

7. Reduce the heat to low and allow to simmer for the next 5 minutes before removing from heat. Serve while still piping hot and enjoy.

(7) Haitian Style Red Snapper

If you are a huge fan of seafood, then this is one of the best recipes you will want to make. For the tastiest results I highly recommend using only the freshest snapper possible.

Serving Sizes: 3 Servings

Cooking Time: 35 Minutes

Ingredient List:

- 3 Red Snappers, Cleaned Thoroughly
- 4 Limes, Fresh and Cut in Half
- 1 Onion, Large in Size and Thinly Sliced
- 1 Pepper, Scotch Bonnet Variety
- 2 teaspoon of Salt, For Taste
- 2 Sprigs of Thyme, Fresh
- 2 Tablespoon of Tomato Paste
- 2 Tablespoon of Oil, Vegetable Variety
- ½ Cup of Vinegar, White in Color
- 3 teaspoon of Spices, Ground Variety
- 2 Cloves of Garlic, Crushed and Minced
- ½ of a Bell Pepper, Green in Color and Finely Diced
- ½ of a Bell Pepper, Red in Color and Finely Diced
- 2 Sprigs of Parsley, Fresh

IIIIIIIIIIIIIIIIIIIIIIIIIIIIIIIIIIIIIIIIIIIIIIIIIIIIIIIIIIIIII

Instructions:

1. Use a small sized container and add in your snapper. Soak your snapper with your vinegar for at least 5 to 10 minutes. After this time rinse your snapper under some running cold water.

2. Scale your snapper and then clean with your limes. Rinse again with some cold water.

3. Squeeze at least one lime over your fish and rub your spices over the surface. Place back into a medium sized container and add in your lime, fresh

thyme, fresh parsley, crushed garlic, chopped bell peppers and onions. Allow to marinate for at least one hour.

4. Then use a large sized skillet and heat up some oil over medium heat. Add in your bell peppers and onions. Cook until translucent before adding in your tomato paste.

5. Add in your seasoned fish along with your water, fresh thyme, fresh parsley and crushed garlic. Allow your mixture to simmer for the next 10 minutes.

6. After this time flip your dish and add in more onions if necessary. Allow to simmer for the next 5 minutes.

7. Remove from heat and serve your fish while still piping hot.

(8) Traditional Haitian Bread

One of the most common types of bread that you will find commonly served in Haiti is this bread. This bread usually comes in a variety of different shapes and sizes and for the tastiest results I highly recommend serving this dish with some traditional Haitian style coffee.

Serving Sizes: 4 Servings

Cooking Time: 3 Hours

Ingredient List:

- 3 ½ Cups of Flour, Bread Variety
- 1 Package of Yeast, Instant and Dry Variety
- 1 ¼ Cup of Water, Warm
- 2 Tablespoon of Sugar, White
- 4 Tablespoon of Butter, Soft
- 1 ½ teaspoon of Salt, For Taste
- 2 Tablespoon of Olive Oil, Extra Virgin Variety

Instructions:

1. The first thing that you will want to do is use a large sized mixing bowl and add in your yeast, sugar, flour and soft butter. Mix thoroughly for the next 3 to 5 minutes.

2. Then add in some water and salt and mix again to combine.

3. Knead your dough by hand until it is smooth to the touch. Once smooth form your dough into a small sized bowl and set aside for later use.

4. Lightly grease a large sized bowl with some olive oil and place your dough ball into this bowl. Cover and allow to rise in a warm place for the next 45 minutes.

5. After this time preheat your oven to 350 degrees. While your oven is heating up grease a counter top with some oil and flatten your dough onto it. Form it into a large sized rectangle.

6. Cut into 4 equal sized pieces. Roll each into a spiral log.

7. Then grease a baking sheet with some olive oil. Place your rolls onto your

pan.

8. Place into your oven to bake for the next 25 to 30 minutes.

9. After this time remove your dough and allow to cool slightly before serving.

(9) Classic Accra

If you are looking for the most traditional and delicious Haitian dish, then this is the perfect dish for you to make. Feel free to fry or bake this classic dish. Either way I know you are going to love this dish.

Serving Sizes: 6 to 8 Servings

Cooking Time: 1 Hour and 10 Minutes

Ingredient List:

- 1 Pound of Malanga, Cut into Small Sized Pieces
- 2 Scallions, Finely Chopped
- 2 Cloves of Garlic, Minced
- 2 Tablespoon of Parsley, Fresh and Finely Chopped
- 1 teaspoon of Thyme, Fresh and Leaves Only
- ¼ teaspoon of Black Pepper, For Taste
- 1 teaspoon of Salt, For Taste
- ½ Tablespoon of Pepper, Scotch Bonnet Variety, Seeded and Finely Chopped
- 1 to 2 Tablespoon of Flour, All Purpose Variety
- 1 Tablespoon of Olive Oil, Extra Virgin Variety
- 2 Cups of Oil, Vegetable Variety

Instructions:

1. Add your malangas into your food processor along with your remaining ingredients except for your oil. Blend on the highest setting until smooth in consistency.

2. Pour your mixture into a medium sized bowl. Cover and allow to marinate for the next 30 minutes.

3. Pour back into your food processor and blend again until smooth in consistency. Place back into your fridge to marinate for another 30 minutes.

4. Remove your mixture from your fridge and allow to come to room temperature.

5. Next add your oil to a large sized skillet and set over medium heat. Once the oil is hot enough add in your mixture by the spoonful and fry until golden brown in color.

6. Place onto a plate lined with paper towels and serve while hot.

(10)   Classic Gateau Au Beurre

This traditional Haitian style cake is used in many classic Haitian style recipes. However, this particular cake recipe is made use rum, giving it a unique and exotic flavor that I know you won't be able to get enough of.

Serving Sizes: 10 to 15 Servings

Cooking Time: 1 Hour and 15 Minutes

Ingredient List:

- 2 Cups of Flour, All Purpose Variety
- 1 ½ Cups of Sugar, White
- 3 Eggs, Large in Size
- 2 Sticks of Butter, Soft
- 3 teaspoons of Baker's Style Baking Powder
- 1, 12 Ounce Can of Milk, Evaporated Variety
- 2 Tablespoon of Rum, Dark in Color and Your Favorite Kind
- 2 teaspoons of Vanilla, Pure
- 1 teaspoon of Lime, Fresh and Zest Only
- 1 teaspoon of Nutmeg
- 2 teaspoons of Salt, For Taste

||||||||||||||||||||||||||||||||||||||||||||||||||||||||||||||||||

Instructions:

1. The first thing that you will want to do is preheat your oven to 350 degrees.

2. While your oven is heating up use a large sized bowl and add in your sugar, eggs, soft butter and fresh lime zest. Use an electric mixer and mix for the next 5 minutes on the lowest speed.

3. Then add in your dark rum, evaporated milk and flour. Use your electric mixer again and beat for the next 5 minutes.

4. After this time add in your salt, baking powder, nutmeg, dash of salt and pure vanilla. Continue to mix for the next 20 minutes or until your mixture is smooth in consistency.

5. Grease a medium sized Bundt pan and fill it halfway with your cake batter.

6. Place your cake into your oven to bake for the next 35 minutes or until your cake is completely baked thorough.

7. Remove your cake from your oven and allow to cool before serving.

(11)   Haitian Style Lambis

This traditional Haitian recipe is made using conch, making it a delicious shellfish recipe that I know you won't be able to get enough of. It is so delicious I know every person in your household will fall in love with.

Serving Sizes: 2 Servings

Cooking Time: 2 Hours and 15 Minutes

Ingredient List:

- 2 Pounds of Lambis, Conch
- 1 Lime, Fresh
- 1 Lemon, Fresh
- 3 Tablespoon of Olive Oil, Extra Virgin Variety
- 2 teaspoons of Vinegar
- 2 Tomatoes, Large in Size and Finely Diced
- 1 Shallot
- 2 Cloves of Garlic, Minced
- 1 Onion, Medium in Size and Minced
- 2 teaspoons of Margarine
- 4 Cups of Water, Warm
- Some Olive Oil, Extra Virgin Variety
- Dash of Hot Sauce, For Taste
- Dash of Black Pepper and Salt, For Taste
- 1 Tablespoon of Tomato Paste

IIIIIIIIIIIIIIIIIIIIIIIIIIIIIIIIIIIIIIIIIIIIIIIIIIIIIIIIIIIIIIIIIII

Instructions:

1. The first thing that you will want to do is clean your conch with your fresh lime and fresh lemon thoroughly.

2. Then place your cleaned conch into a medium sized saucepan with your water.

3. Cook over low heat for the next 2 hours or until tender to the touch. During

this time make sure that you skim the foam off of the top and reserve your broth.

4. Next use a large sized skillet and set over medium heat. Add in your conch and brown thoroughly in some oil, your margarine and a few drops of your fresh lime juice.

5. Add in your onions, shallot, dash of salt and pepper, tomato paste, hot sauce, vinegar, garlic and tomatoes. Stir thoroughly to combine.

6. Ad in your broth and allow to simmer for the next 10 minutes.

7. Season with some salt and pepper before removing from heat. Serve whenever you are ready and enjoy.

(12)   Haitian Pate

This filling beef patty is served up in many places around the Caribbean and is made using various meats such as beef, pork or chicken. Feel free to serve this dish up as a delicious appetizer during your next dinner gathering.

Serving Sizes: 12 Servings

Cooking Time: 1 Hour

Ingredient List:

- 1 Pound of Beef, Lean and Ground
- 1 Onion, Small In Size and Finely Diced
- ½ of a Pepper, Scotch Bonnet Variety and Minced
- 1 teaspoon of Lime Juice, Fresh
- 2 Tablespoon of Tomato Paste
- 1 teaspoon of Adobo Seasoning
- 1 Tablespoon of Olive Oil, Extra Virgin Variety
- 1 Egg, Large in Size
- 1 Tablespoon of Water, Warm
- 1 pack of Puff Pastry Sheets
- ¼ Cup of Haitian Seasoning
- 1 teaspoon of Vinegar

Instructions:

1. The first thing that you will want to do is set your puff pastry sheets aside to thaw completely. This should take at least 30 minutes.

2. Then use a medium sized bowl and mix together your meat, Haitian seasoning, adobo seasoning and vinegar until thoroughly mixed.

3. Use a large sized skillet and place it over medium to high heat. Once the oil is hot enough add in your beef and cook until brown in color. This should take at least 10 minutes.

4. Next add in your tomato paste along with your bonnet pepper. Mix again to combine and reduce the heat to low.

5. Then preheat your oven to 350 degrees.

6. Unfold your puff pastry sheet onto a lightly floured surface and flatten with a rolling pin. Cut your sheets into 6 equal sized rectangles.

7. Add a spoonful of your meat right into the center of your rectangles and fold your pastry over to cover. Seal the edges with a fork and place onto a lightly greased baking sheet.

8. Next use a small sized bowl and mix together your egg with your tablespoon of water until evenly mixed. Brush your rectangles with this egg wash.

9. Place into your oven to bake for the next 20 to 25 minutes or until golden brown in color.

10. After this time remove from oven and allow to cool slightly before serving.

(13)   Delicious Haitian Style Meatballs

Who doesn't love meatballs? Well, if you are a huge fan of Haitian food and love classic meatballs, then this is the perfect dish for you to make. These meatballs are dredge in flour and fried to perfection, making it perfect for those looking for a filling meal to enjoy.

Serving Sizes: 4 Servings

Cooking Time: 20 Minutes

Ingredient List:

- 1 ½ Pounds of Beef, Ground and Lean
- 1 teaspoon of Salt, For Taste and Seasoned Variety
- ½ teaspoon of Salt, For Taste
- ½ teaspoon of Onion, Powdered Variety
- 2 to 3 Cloves of Garlic, Minced
- ¼ Cup of Bell Peppers, Minced
- ¼ Cup of Onion, Minced
- 2 Tablespoon of Epis
- 2 to 3 Tablespoon of Pikliz, Juice Only
- 2 Slices of Bread, Soaked
- 1/3 Cup of Flour, All Purpose Variety
- 1 ½ Cup of Olive Oil, Extra Virgin Variety

IIIIIIIIIIIIIIIIIIIIIIIIIIIIIIIIIIIIIIIIIIIIIIIIIIIIIIIIIIIIIIIII

Instructions:

1. Use a large sized bowl and add in your lean beef, minced peppers, minced onions, minced garlic, epis, powdered onion, powdered garlic and Pikliz. Stir thoroughly to combine.

2. Once your mixture has been mixed, roll your mixture into small sized even meatballs.

3. Coat each of your meatballs with some flour.

4. Then add your oil into a medium sized skillet and heat over medium heat. Once your oil is hot enough add in your meatballs and cook until thoroughly

brown in color.

5. Once fully cooked drain your meatballs on a plate lined with paper towels. Serve while still warm and enjoy.

(14)   Healthy Beet Salad

If you are looking for something on the healthier side, then this is the perfect salad dish for you to make. It is bright in color and make for some of the most delicious salad recipe you will ever come across.

Serving Sizes: 8 Servings

Cooking Time: 30 Minutes

Ingredient List:

- 4 Potatoes, Red in Color
- 2 Beets, Fresh
- 1 Stalk of Celery, Finely Diced
- ½ of an Onion, Finely Diced
- ½ of a Bell Pepper, Green in Color and Finely Diced
- ½ Cup of Mayonnaise, Your Favorite Kind
- ½ teaspoon of Pepper, For Taste
- ½ teaspoon of Salt, For Taste
- 1 Carrot, Large in Size, Fresh and Finely Diced

Instructions:

1. First bring a large sized pot over medium heat. Add in some water and bring to a boil. Once boiling add in your beets and allow to boil for the next 5 minutes.

2. Next add your potatoes into your pot and continue to boil for the next 5 minutes.

3. Add in your carrots and continue to boil for another 5 minutes.

4. After this time drain your potatoes, carrots and beets and allow to cool enough for you to handle.

5. Once cool dice your ingredients finely and add them to a large sized mixing bowl along with your remaining ingredients. Stir thoroughly to combine.

6. Cover with some plastic wrap and place into your fridge to chill completely. Serve while cold and enjoy.

(15)   Classic Potato Bread

This classic Potato bread recipe is a common dessert dish that every Haitian loves. It is the consistency of banana bread, making this the perfect dessert dish to make to impress your friends and family.

Serving Sizes: 8 to 10 Servings

Cooking Time: 2 Hours

Ingredient List:

- 2 ½ Cups of Sweet Potatoes, Peeled and Washed
- 1 Cup of Milk, Evaporated
- 1 ¼ Cup of Milk, Coconut Variety
- 1 Cup of Brown Sugar, Light and Packed
- ¼ Cup of Butter, Soft
- 2 Tablespoon of Vanilla, Pure
- 1 Banana, Ripe
- 1 teaspoon of Cinnamon, Ground
- 1 teaspoon of Nutmeg
- 1 Lime, Zest Only
- ½ teaspoon of Salt, For Taste
- 1 Tablespoon of Ginger, Ground
- ½ Cup of Raisins, Your Favorite Kind
- ¼ Cup of Rum, Dark and Optional

IIIIIIIIIIIIIIIIIIIIIIIIIIIIIIIIIIIIIIIIIIIIIIIIIIIIIIIII

Instructions:

1. The first thing that you will want to do is soak your raisins in your dark rum. If you are not using rum, use water instead.

2. Once soaked add to a pan and add in your evaporated milk, coconut milk, light and packed brown sugar, soft butter, dash of salt and nutmeg. Stir thoroughly to combine.

3. Cook this mixture over low to medium heat and mash with a fork as you do so.

4. Next mash your bananas, lime zest and ground ginger and add to your cooking mixture. Reduce the heat to low and stir thoroughly to combine.

5. After about 40 minutes add in your vanilla and stir again. Cover and allow to simmer for the next 5 to 10 minutes or until soft to the touch.

6. Pour your mixture into a generously greased baking dish.

7. Place into your oven to bake at 350 degrees for the next hour and 30 minutes or until golden in color.

8. After this time remove and allow to cool completely before placing into your fridge to chill for the next 24 hours or until your cake becomes the consistency of cake. Serve whenever you are ready and enjoy.

(16)   Healthy Haitian Style Avocado Salad

Here is yet another simple salad recipe that I know you are going to fall in love with. Feel free to serve this dish as a tasty appetizer or side dish. For the tastiest results I highly recommend serving this dish with some fried plantains.

Serving Sizes: 2 to 4 Servings

Cooking Time: 10 Minutes

Ingredient List:

- 2 Avocados, Peeled and Cut into Small Sized Squares
- 1 Onion, Finely Chopped
- ½ of a Lime, Juice Only
- 1 teaspoon of Olive Oil, Extra Virgin Variety
- ½ teaspoon of Pepper, For Taste
- ½ teaspoon of Salt, For Taste

Instructions:

1. First slice up your avocados and cut them into small sized square pieces. Place into a medium sized bowl.

2. Finely chop your onions and add them to your bowl.

3. Add in your fresh lime juice, dash of salt and pepper and mix thoroughly to combine.

4. Serve this dish right away and enjoy.

(17)   Haitian Style Beef Stew

Here is yet another stew recipe that I know you are going to want to make over and over again. It is the perfect dish to make for when you are looking for a filling and warm recipe to make during the cold winter months.

Serving Sizes: 6 to 8 Servings

Cooking Time: 1 Hour and 30 Minutes

Ingredient List:

- 1 Pound of Beef, Cut into Small Cubes
- 2 Limes, Fresh and Cut in Half
- 1 Onion, Large in Size and Finely Chopped
- 4 Scallions
- 4 Cloves of Garlic, Crushed
- 2 Tablespoon of Salt, For Taste
- ½ Tablespoon of Black Pepper, For Taste
- 2 Cloves, Whole
- 2 Bay Leaves, Fresh
- 2 Sprigs of Parsley, Fresh and Roughly Chopped
- 1 Sprig of Thyme, Fresh
- 2 Carrots, Peeled and Thinly Sliced
- 2 Sticks of Celery
- 1 Malanga, Cut into Small Sized Chunks
- 2 Plantains, Fresh
- 1 Yucca
- 10 Ounces of Spinach, Fresh and Baby Variety

Ingredients for Your Dumplings:

- 2 Cups of Flour, Whole Wheat Variety
- 1 Tablespoon of Olive Oil, Extra Virgin Variety
- 1 teaspoon of All Spice
- 1 teaspoon of Nutmeg

- 1 teaspoon of Cayenne Pepper
- ½ Cups of Water, Warm

IIIIIIIIIIIIIIIIIIIIIIIIIIIIIIIIIIIIIIIIIIIIIIIIIIIIIIIIIIIIIIIIIIIIIIII

Instructions:

1. First marinate your beef with your scallions, garlic, salt and dash of pepper for at least one hour in your fridge.

2. While your beef is marinating, make your dumplings. To do this mix all of your dumpling ingredients together in a large sized bowl. Once mix shape into small sized balls and set aside for later use.

3. Then use a large sized pot and add in your marinated beef. Cook over medium heat until thoroughly brown in color.

4. Once browned add in your water, bay leaves, fresh parsley, fresh thyme and cloves. Stir thoroughly to combine and allow to cook at a low simmer for the next 40 minutes. During the time make sure that you stir your mixture occasionally.

5. After this time add in 3 quarts of water and allow your stew to come to a boil.

6. Once boiling add in your carrots, celery, fresh plantains, yucca, baby spinach and Malanga. Stir again to combine and continue to cook for the next 20 minutes.

7. After this time add in your dumplings and allow to simmer for the next 20 minutes, making sure to stir occasionally.

8. Remove from heat and serve whenever you are ready.

(18)   Simple Boiled Plantains

Boiled plantains are often served with many meals in Haiti. These fruits are available all year long and can be used to make a variety of side dishes similar to this one. For the tastiest results I highly recommend serving this dish alongside a delicious Haitian inspired meal.

Serving Sizes: 1 Serving

Cooking Time: 25 Minutes

Ingredient List:

- 3 Cups of Water, Warm
- 1 Plantain, Green in Color
- 1 teaspoon of Salt, For Taste

IIIIIIIIIIIIIIIIIIIIIIIIIIIIIIIIIIIIIIIIIIIIIIIIIIIIIIIIIIIIIIIIIIII

Instructions:

1. Place your water and salt into a small sized pot and set over medium to high heat. Bring your water to a boil.

2. Then rinse your plantain thoroughly under some cold water.

3. Cut off at least 1 inch off the ends of the plantain.

4. Use a knife and score the skin of your plantain from end to end. Cut your plantain in half and add to your pot.

5. Allow your plantain to boil for at least 20 minutes.

6. After this time remove your plantain from the water and remove the skin. Serve while warm and enjoy.

(19)   Haitian Style Chicken Smothered in Sauce

Here is a classic chicken dish straight from the streets of Haiti that I know you are going to fall in love with. Feel free to add whatever ingredients you like to this dish to truly make it unique.

Serving Sizes: 4 Servings

Cooking Time: 45 Minutes

Ingredient List:

- 1 Onion, Large in Size and Thinly Sliced
- 1 Pepper, Scotch Bonnet Variety and Chopped Finely
- 3 Cloves of Garlic, Minced
- ¾ Cup of Tomato Sauce
- 3 Tablespoon of Sugar, White in Color
- Dash of Salt, For Taste
- 2 to 3 Limes, Fresh
- Some Oil, Vegetable Variety

Instructions:

1. The first thing that you will want to do is wash your chicken well and pat dry with a paper towel.

2. Once dried rub each piece of your chicken with your limes and season with a dash of salt.

3. Next heat up some oil in an oven safe dish. Then preheat your oven to 375 degrees.

4. Heat up some oil in a large sized skillet placed over medium heat. Once it is hot enough fry up your chicken until cooked completely.

5. Next use a medium sized bowl and add in your garlic, sugar, tomato sauce and dash of salt. Stir well to combine. Add into your baking dish along with your chicken.

6. Place into your oven to bake for the next 20 minutes or until your chicken is cooked completely.

7. Remove from oven and allow to cool slightly before serving.

(20)   Hearty Black Mushroom Rice

This dish is often considered to be a delicacy in many parts of Haiti. While it is not usually served every day in that country, once you get a taste of it yourself, I know you are going to want to make it over and over again.

Serving Sizes: 4 Servings

Cooking Time: 45 Minutes

Ingredient List:

- 2 Cups of Mushrooms, Dried and Black Variety
- 3 Cloves of Garlic, Minced
- 2 Tablespoon of Olive Oil, Extra Virgin Variety
- 1 Onion, Small in Size and Finely Chopped
- 2 Cups of Rice, Long Grain Variety
- 2 teaspoons of Salt, For Taste
- 1 teaspoon of Cloves, Ground
- 1, 12 Ounce Can of Lime Beans
- 1 to 2 Sprigs of Thyme, Fresh
- 1 Pepper, Cotch Bonnet Variety and Green in Color

IIIIIIIIIIIIIIIIIIIIIIIIIIIIIIIIIIIIIIIIIIIIIIIIIIIIIIIIIIIIIIII

Instructions:

1. Use a small sized pot and add in at least 4 cups of water. Add in your mushrooms and allow to soak for the next 10 minutes.

2. Increase the heat to high and allow your mushrooms to boil for the next 10 minutes.

3. After this time strain your mushroom water into another container to use later on. Toss out your mushrooms.

4. Then use a large sized pot and set over medium heat. Once it is hot enough add in your garlic and onions and cook for the next 2 minutes.

5. Add in your rice and stir to combine. Continue to cook for the next 5 minutes before adding in your mushrooms water, dash of salt, cloves and canned lima beans.

6. Bring this mixture to a boil before reducing the heat to low. Allow to cook for the next 10 to 15 minutes or until most of your water evaporates.

7. Stir quickly before adding in your thyme and pepper.

8. Cover and allow to continue cooking over low heat for the next 15 minutes.

9. After this time remove from heat and serve whenever you are ready.

(21)   Traditional Pork Griot

Here is a delicious dinner recipe that I know you won't be able to get enough of. Packed full of a sour, sweet and addictive flavor, I am confident you are going to want to make this dish over and over again.

Serving Sizes: 4 to 5 Servings

Cooking Time: 2 Hours and 45 Minutes

Ingredient List:

- 1, 3 Pound of Pork Shoulder, Cut into Small Sized Pieces
- 1 to 3 Limes, Fresh and Juice Only
- 2 to 3 Tablespoon of Parsley, Fresh and Roughly Chopped
- 2 teaspoons of Garlic, Minced
- 2 teaspoons of Thyme, Fresh
- 2 Stalks of Scallions, Finely Chopped
- ½ teaspoon of Pepper, White in Color and Ground
- ½ of an Onion, Medium in Size and Thinly Sliced
- 1 Pepper, Scotch Bonnet Variety and Optional
- 1 Bell Pepper, Red in Color and Finely Chopped
- 1 teaspoon of Paprika, Smoked Variety
- 1 Tablespoon of Chicken Bouillon, Powdered Variety
- 1 ½ teaspoon of Salt, For Taste

IIIIIIIIIIIIIIIIIIIIIIIIIIIIIIIIIIIIIIIIIIIIIIIIIIIIIIIIIIIIIIIIIIIII

Instructions:

1. The first thing that you will want to do is place your pork into a large sized bowl.

2. Add in all of your remaining ingredients and stir thoroughly to coat.

3. Allow your pork to marinate in your bowl for the next 2 hours or overnight preferably.

4. After this time place your mixture into a large sized pot placed over medium heat.

5. Bring to a boil and reduce the heat to low once boiling and allow to simmer for the next hour or until tender to the touch.

6. After this time remove from heat and serve while still piping hot. Enjoy.

(22)   Hearty Black Bean Soup

If you are looking for something on the heartier and warmer side to warm you up once the weather begins to grow cold, then this is the perfect dish for you to make. For the tastiest results I highly recommend serving this dish up with some white rice.

Serving Sizes: 8 Servings

Cooking Time: 1 Hour and 35 Minutes

Ingredient List:

- 1, 16 Ounce Bag of Black Beans
- 1 Cup of Milk, Coconut Variety
- 1 Tablespoon of Salt, For Taste
- 1 Tablespoon of Pepper, For Taste
- 1 Tablespoon of Olive Oil, Extra Virgin Variety
- 1 teaspoon of Cloves, Ground
- 1 Cube of Chicken Bouillon
- 8 Cups of Water, Warm

IIIIIIIIIIIIIIIIIIIIIIIIIIIIIIIIIIIIIIIIIIIIIIIIIIIIIIIIIIIIII

Instructions:

1. Use a large sized pot and boil your water and beans together over medium heat for the next hour or until tender to the touch.

2. Once tender add at least ¾ cup of beans to a blender and blend on the highest setting until smooth in consistency.

3. Strain your puree and return the mixture to your pot.

4. Add in your oil, milk, dash of salt and pepper and cube of chicken bouillon. Stir thoroughly to combine.

5. Continue to cook for the next 15 minutes before removing from heat and serving.

(23)   Haitian Style Potato Salad

If you are bored of traditional potato salad, then this is one dish you are certainly going to want to make. Feel free to add whatever vegetables you wish to make this dish truly unique.

Serving Sizes: 4 to 6 Servings

Cooking Time: 35 Minutes

Ingredient List:

- 4 Potatoes, Peeled and Cut into Small Sized Cubes
- 1 Carrot, Fresh, Peeled and Minced
- 2 ¼ teaspoon of Salt, For Taste
- 1 Beet, Small in Size and Fresh
- 2 Eggs, Large in Size
- ½ Cup of Peas, Sweet Variety, Frozen and Thawed
- ½ of an Onion, Large in Size and Minced
- 1/3 Cup of Bell Pepper, Red in Color and Finely Diced
- 1/3 Cup of Bell Pepper, Green in Color and Finely Diced
- 2 Tablespoon of Mayonnaise, Your Favorite Kind
- ¼ teaspoon of Black Pepper, For Taste
- Dash of Salt, For Taste

IIIIIIIIIIIIIIIIIIIIIIIIIIIIIIIIIIIIIIIIIIIIIIIIIIIIIIIIIIIIIIIIIII

Instructions:

1. The first thing that you will want to do is boil your potatoes and carrots in some water with a dash of salt over medium heat. Boil for the next 10 minutes or until tender to the touch.

2. Then use a separate medium sized pot and boil your beets over medium heat with some salt for the next 10 minutes or until tender to the touch. Once tender peel and dice the beets finely.

3. Boil your eggs in a separate small sized pot with some water for at least 10 minutes. After this time cool, peel the shells and chop finely.

4. Use a large sized bowl and add in your potatoes, beet, chopped eggs, sweet

peas, fresh carrots, onions, green and red peppers and mayonnaise.

5. Stir thoroughly to combine before add in your black pepper.

6. Season with a dash of salt and pepper and serve whenever you are ready.

(24)   Asiago Shrimp Pasta

If you are a huge fan of seafood, this is one dish that you need to make for yourself. It is the perfect dish to make if you are looking for something on the classier side and that will surely impress your friends and family.

Serving Sizes: 2 Servings

Cooking Time: 30 Minutes

Ingredient List:

- 1 Pound of Angel Hair Pasta, Whole Grain Variety, Cooked and Drained
- 3 Tablespoon of Olive Oil, Extra Virgin Variety
- 2 Tablespoon of Butter, Unsalted Variety and Soft
- 1 Tablespoon of Salt, For Taste
- ½ Tablespoon of Pepper, For Taste
- ½ Tablespoon of Red Pepper Flakes
- 6 Cloves of Garlic, Thinly Sliced
- ½ Tablespoon of Parsley, Dried
- ¼ Tablespoon of Oregano, Dried
- ¼ Tablespoon of Thyme, Dried
- ½ Cup of Rum, Dark in Color and Your Favorite Kind
- 1 ½ Cups of Asiago Cheese, Finely Shredded
- 1 Pound of Shrimp, Jumbo Variety, Peeled and Deveined
- Some Cilantro, Fresh and for Garnish

IIIIIIIIIIIIIIIIIIIIIIIIIIIIIIIIIIIIIIIIIIIIIIIIIIIIIIIIIIIII

Instructions:

1. Use a large sized skillet and heat up your olive oil. Once the oil is hot enough add in your butter and garlic. Cook until your garlic is fragrant.

2. Then add in your dash of salt and pepper, red pepper flakes, parsley, fresh oregano and fresh thyme. Cook for the next 2 to 3 minutes, making sure to stir thoroughly.

3. Add in your rum, but make sure you do so away from direct heat. Allow to

cook until your rum is reduced by at least half.

4. Add in your shrimp and allow to cool thoroughly until no longer pink.

5. Remove from heat and add in your cheese and angel hair pasta. Garnish with your cilantro and serve while still piping hot.

(25)   Haitian Griot II

Here's another griot adaptation that I know you are going to want to make over and over again. This particular recipe is classier than the other one in this book, but nonetheless it is as delicious as you will find.

Serving Sizes: 4 Servings

Cooking Time: 3 Hours and 5 Minutes

Ingredient List:

- 1 Pound of Pork Shoulder, Cut into Small Sized Cubes
- 1 Lime, Fresh and Cut Into Halves
- 1 teaspoon of Sea Salt, For Taste

Ingredients for Your Marinade:

- 2 Oranges, Fresh and Juice Only
- 2 Limes, Fresh and Juice Only
- 4 Cloves of Garlic, Minced
- 2 Shallots, Finely Diced
- 1 Pepper, Habanero Variety, Deseeded and Minced
- 1 Handful of Parsley, Fresh and Roughly Chopped
- 1 Handful of Thyme, Fresh, Stems Removed and Minced
- 1 teaspoon of Sea Salt, For Taste
- 1 teaspoon of Black Pepper, For Taste

Ingredients for Your Malice:

- Leftover marinade from your griot
- 1 Tablespoon of Honey, Raw
- 1 Tablespoon of Mustard, Dijon Variety
- 1 teaspoon of Sea Salt, For Taste
- 1 teaspoon of Black Pepper, For Taste

Instructions:

1. To start place your pork in an empty bowl.

2. Then use a medium sized bowl and add your lime and sea salt over your pork. Rub leftover lime pulp over your pork. Then rinsed your pork over your cold water and set aside for later use.

3. Add your pork into a large sized Dutch oven along with your cloves of garlic, onions, shallots, pepper, fresh parsley and fresh thyme.

4. Add in your orange and lime juice. Stir well to combine and massage juice into your marinade. Season with a dash of salt and pepper and allow to marinate for the next hour.

5. After this time preheat your oven to 350 degrees. Then place your pot with your pork and marinade over high heat to bring your mixture to a boil. Once boiling quickly transfer to your oven with a cover to bake for the next 1 hour and 30 minutes.

6. After this time remove oven and place back onto your stock. Spoon out your pork and place onto a baking sheet. Then pour your marinade through a strainer to remove any solids. Pour your smooth marinade back into your pot.

7. Place your pot over low to medium heat and allow to simmer for the next 20 minutes or until your mixture reduces.

8. Preheat your oven to a high broil.

9. Place your pork pieces into your oven to broil for at least 5 minutes on each side or until nicely charred.

10. Remove from oven and serve with your reduced sauce drizzled over the top. Garnish with some parsley and enjoy right away.

Author's Afterthoughts

Thank you for making the decision to invest in one of my cookbooks! I cherish all my readers and hope you find joy in preparing these meals as I have.

There are so many books available and I am truly grateful that you decided to buy this one and follow it from beginning to end.

Made in the USA
Columbia, SC
10 December 2024

48862822R00031